Contents

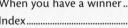

Learn **How to Buy and Sell on eBay for 5 Bucks**

Stephen Gregory, Larry Becker, and Jim Workman

Fair Shake Press, an imprint of Pearson Technology Group, division of Pearson Education

Composed in the typeface Cronos MM from Adobe Systems

ISBN 0-321-28784-3

9 8 7 6 5 4 3 2 1

Printed and bound in the United States of America

"Yeah, I'd pay five bucks to learn more about that...."

- *Learn the iPod for 5 Bucks* ISBN 0321287851
- *Learn How to Buy and Sell on eBay for 5 Bucks* ISBN 0321287843
- *Learn the Canon EOS Digital Rebel Camera for 5 Bucks* ISBN 0321287827
- *Learn the Nikon Coolpix Camera for 5 Bucks* ISBN 0321287835
- *Learn How to Make Great Digital Photos for 5 Bucks* ISBN 032130361X
- *Learn the Low-Carb Lifestyle for 5 Bucks* ISBN 0321303601
- *Learn How to Win at Poker for 5 Bucks* ISBN 0321287819

Look for these terrific little books in all kinds of stores, everywhere. Lots more neat little "books for people who hate reading the manual" are on the way.

Keep checking **www.fairshakepress.com**. We'd love to hear what you'd pay five bucks to learn more about...

FairShake press

How to use this book

Welcome to a new way of learning high-tech services. This book is different because it's designed for one thing—to teach you just what you need to know, and nothing more, about how to buy and sell on Bay.

You're not going to learn all the inside details, the inner workings of eBay, their history, or a bunch of highly advanced techniques. This just isn't that kind of book. Instead, we cover the basics, the "meat and potatoes," to get you buying and selling fast on eBay. As you're surely aware, eBay is a sprawling site with hundreds of thousands of pages—it's absolutely amazing what you can find there. So how do you make eBay simple? How do you make it so anyone can start browsing, buying, or selling?

We came up with a way to make eBay so simple to learn, so simple to use, and so much fun that you'll be able to start using it right away—today—and best of all you'll love it. We basically left off all the extra stuff and skipped all the techno-jargon and geeky stuff. We only cover the most requested, most important, and most useful aspects of using eBay so you can start having fun with it right away.

The book is organized assuming that you've never used eBay before (or that if you did, you didn't get very far), so we start with how to look around and find interesting items for sale, and then how to set things up so you can bid on auctions yourself. In the second part of the book, we show you how you can sell your own items on eBay (that takes a little more effort, but honestly, just a little). Before you know it, you'll be holding Dutch auctions and watching the money roll in. What's a Dutch auction? You're about to find out.

So turn on your computer, log on to www.eBay.com, turn the page, and start learning how to use the world's largest online auction site. You're going to have a blast!

—*Stephen Gregory, Larry Becker, and Jim Workman*

Becoming a member of eBay (it's free!)

> *If you're thinking of buying or selling, this is your first step*

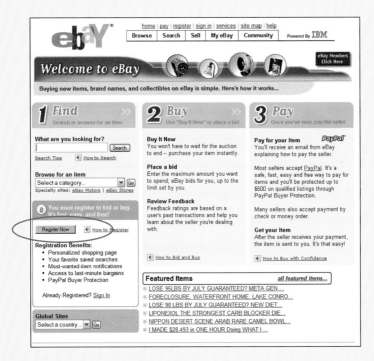

In order to actually buy and sell items on eBay, you have to register to become an eBay member. Luckily, it's easy. Just to www.eBay.com*, and click on the Register Now button (as shown above) to jump to the Registration page and start the registration process.

*U.K. residents see www.eBay.co.uk

Create your eBay User ID

susiewah

Example: rose789 (Don't use your email address)
Your User ID identifies you to other eBay users.

Create password

••••••

6 character minimum

Enter a password that's easy for you to remember, but hard for others to guess. **See tips.**

Re-enter password

••••••

Secret question   Secret answer

What is your school's mascot?   Gator

You will be asked for the answer to your secret question if you forget your password.

Date of birth

September 24 Year 1980

Continue >

When the Registration page appears, it just asks you the usual stuff—name, address, city, etc. But there is one portion of the Registration page that requires some thought—choosing your eBay User ID and password. It requires some thought because the password you probably want to use (your name) is almost undoubtedly taken, since there are so many millions of people already using eBay. Your User ID is important because it allows you to identify yourself to the auction and because it's unique, it keeps others using your identity. So come up with your own ID name and password. (If the ID name you entered is already taken by someone else, when you click the Continue button it will ask you to try a different ID. In fact, it will even suggest one for you, if you like.)

> *This is how eBay communicates with you*

You're almost done.

To complete eBay registration, just click the button below:

Complete eBay Registration >

This will confirm that your email is working.

Because eBay communicates with you via email (in fact, you can't open your account without one, because for safety reasons eBay sends you a confirmation email that requires you to respond), you have to enter your email address. Some people like to create a separate email account just for their eBay auction communication (rather than having it go their personal or company email). If you'd like to do this, both Yahoo and Hotmail offer free email accounts—all you have to do is stop by and sign up with them. Now, back to eBay: once you enter your email address and agree to the eBay terms of membership, go check your email for the confirmation notice sent by eBay. Click the "Complete eBay Registration" button that appears within your email (as shown above), and it will send you right back to eBay, where you'll automatically be signed in.

Signing in is optional when you're just looking

> *But if you want to buy something you'll need to sign in*

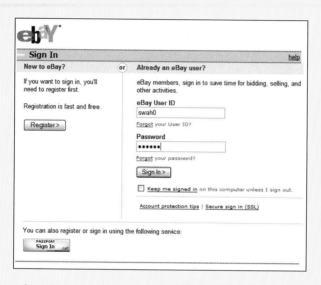

If you just want to start searching for items, you can go to the Home page and look around using any of the browsing or search methods eBay offers (we'll cover those in a minute). However, if you think you might want to bid on an item, you may as well sign in with your new User ID and password. (If you're following this book step-by-step you're already signed in.) At the top of eBay's Home page you'll see a Sign In link. Click there and enter your ID and password on the page that opens (shown above). Signing in doesn't commit you to buying anything or placing a bid, it just lets eBay know who you are and enables you to bid if the mood strikes you.

Start searching with the Browse feature

> *We'll show you where to start...*

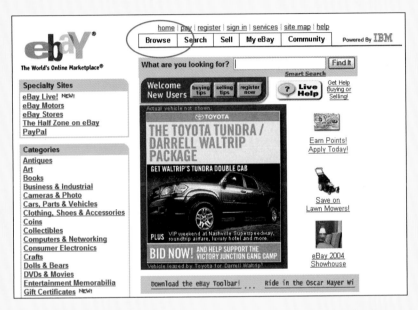

There are several ways to search for things on eBay; as you get further into this, you may find you prefer one search method over another, but for now, let's start with browsing. Click on the Browse button at the top of the page (it's circled in red above), which takes you to the Browse page (shown on the next page).

> *You can search everywhere, or just within specific categories*

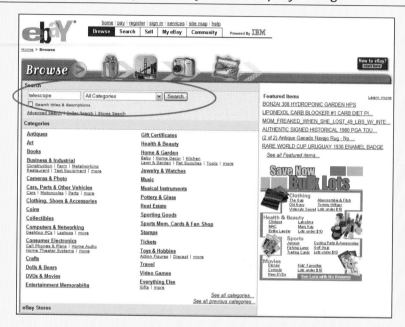

When you click the Browse button you'll be taken to the main Browse page (shown above). This page contains a list of popular categories to help you find what you're looking for faster. For example, if you're looking for a telescope, you might click on the Cameras & Photo category link, which will take you to a page that lists links to different types of photography-related auctions (including telescopes). If you want a much broader search, you can use the Search field near the top of the page (it's circled above in red). There's a pop-up menu beside the Search field, and if you leave it set to the default of "All Categories," it will search all of eBay, rather than just within a specific category, so you can expect to get some toy telescopes in your search results. To narrow your search, choose a category from the pop-up list.

Narrowing your search

> If a regular search brings you too many responses, try narrowing it a bit

I f you want to refine your search from the very beginning, instead of clicking Browse, click the Search button (to the right of Browse). You will see a text field where you can enter the name of the item you are looking for or some keywords about the item. There are also several pop-up menus that allow you to further refine your search. When you get used to using these tools (think of them as "search limiters") you'll be able to find the exact items you want much more quickly. Obviously, the more modifiers you add to a search, the fewer items you'll get back as a result, but it's more likely the results will be just what you're looking for. Try doing a search here a couple of times and you'll get the hang of it.

Understanding your search results

> *OK, your search came back with some results—but what does it all mean?*

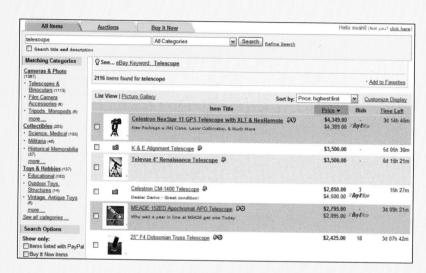

Our search for telescopes returned 2116 results (the first six are shown in the main box above). The results usually show a small photo for each item, followed by the item's name (underlined and in dark blue because the name is a live link to that item). To the right of each item is the current bid price (someone has said they're willing to pay that much for it), the number of bids on that item, and the length of time remaining on that auction (in days, hours and minutes). To find out more about one of the items listed in your search results, just click on the link (you're not bidding on the item—just looking).

> *You can have eBay list the products in the order you prefer*

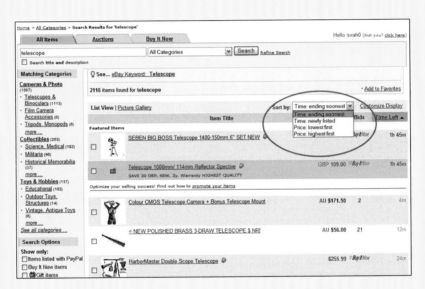

Bay has provided a nifty feature to help you sift through your search results—the "Sort by" option. For example, let's say you're looking for a really cheap telescope. You can change the "Sort by" option to "Sort by Price: lowest first" and then your results will be resorted by price, showing you the lowest-priced telescopes first. You do this by choosing a sorting option from the "Sort by" pop-up menu at the top right of the main results box (it's shown circled above). Other "Sort by" choices include: Price: highest first; Time: ending soonest, and Time: newly listed.

> *The auction ends at 6:47 p.m. but in which time zone?*

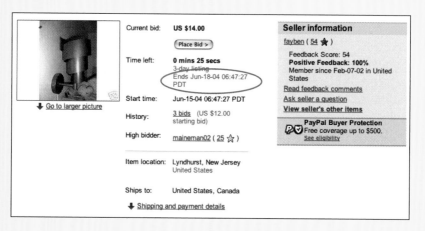

Current bid:	**US $14.00**
	(Place Bid >)
Time left:	**0 mins 25 secs**
	3-day listing
	Ends Jun-18-04 06:47:27 PDT
Start time:	Jun-15-04 06:47:27 PDT
History:	3 bids (US $12.00 starting bid)
High bidder:	mainman02 (25 ☆)
Item location:	Lyndhurst, New Jersey United States
Ships to:	United States, Canada

⬇ Shipping and payment details

⬇ Go to larger picture

Seller information

fayben (54 ⭐)

Feedback Score: 54
Positive Feedback: 100%
Member since Feb-07-02 in United States

Read feedback comments
Ask seller a question
View seller's other items

PayPal Buyer Protection
Free coverage up to $500.
See eligibility

Because people bid on items all over the country (and all over the world for that matter) when it says an auction ends at 6:47 p.m., is that 6:47 p.m. New York time? California time? London time? Actually, it's 6:47 p.m. eBay time (which is Pacific time, based on the location of eBay's headquarters in San Jose, California). So how do eBay pros make sure they don't miss out on placing last-minute bids for items? They set their computer clocks to match eBay's Pacific Time Zone. That way, if they're on the East Coast they don't miss every auction's ending time by three hours. If that seems a bit extreme, then just remember to keep in mind that all auction ending times are on California time.

☐	Nikon D70 Digital SLR Super Kit With 3 Pro Lenses+$2500 Just Released & In Stock Must See! Huge Kit!!!	**$1,648.99** - $1,699.99 ≡Buy It Now	4h 34m
☐	Nikon D70 D100 D2H D1X F5 F100 N80 N75 Pro Grip Strap 🖼️🔖	**$22.95** - $24.95 ≡Buy It Now	4h 34m
☐	Nikon AF Nikkor 28-70mm 3.5-4.5 D D70 F100 F5 D100 D1 🖼️🔖	**$26.00** 5	4h 51m
☐	Nikon D70 Digital SLR with 18-70mm & 47st Deluxe Kit! 🖼️🔖	**$1,579.95** - $1,589.95 ≡Buy It Now	4h 58m
☐	NIKON D70 DIGITAL SLR PRO MONSTER PK+LOTS OF EXTRAS!!! 🖼️🔖	**$1,549.99** ≡Buy It Now	5h 11m
☐	Nikon EN-EL3 ENEL3 Li-Ion Battery D100 D70 1350mAh 🖼️🔖	**$9.99** 1	5h 30m

Some search results will show a second price with the words "Buy It Now" appearing after it. This is letting you know that if you really want the item, and want it now (and you're willing to forego the possible savings if you win the auction with a low bid), you can bypass the whole auction and simply purchase the item for the amount shown right before the words "Buy it Now." To buy it now, just click on the item's description, and when you get to the item's page, you'll see a "Buy it Now" button. Click on that button and it will ask you how many you want. (Hey, if you can buy it now, they probably have more than one in stock, right?) It gives you the firm price, then if you really want to buy it now, click Continue.

> *First you have to find out what the seller will accept for payment*

Payment methods accepted

This seller, **prefers PayPal**.

• PayPal® (VISA, cards)

• Personal check
• Money order/Cashiers check
• Other - See Payment Instructions for payment methods accepted
• Visa/MasterCard, Discover
Learn about payment methods.

eBay recommended services

Increase your PayPal sending limit. Get Verified today.

Each person selling an item on eBay lists which forms of payment they'll accept. Before you bid on an item, it's important to see if you have the form of payment they'll accept. (For example, it would be a shame to win an auction only to later find out that the seller accepts only VISA, and you only have the Discover Card, so make sure check this out before you place a bid.) To find out what the seller accepts, click on the Shipping and Payment Details link that appears at the bottom of the item's auction page or just keep scrolling down the page and eventually you'll find the Payment methods accepted area (shown above). The seller will list the forms of payment they accept (which credit cards, if any, whether they accept personal checks, money orders/cashiers checks, or PayPal (see page 20).

Before you click the "Place Bid" button

> *There's important information on an item's description page*

When you find something you want, click the link to view the details for that item; that's where the Place Bid button lives. Before you click Place Bid, we recommend taking a moment to look over some of the information listed about the item. You'll find the history, current bid, highest bidder (and how many auctions this person has won), the eBay item number (something you'll need if you bid), seller info (items they've sold, positive and negative feedback), and which forms of payment they'll accept (will they take a personal check?). Finally, this is a good time to check the photos for visible flaws and look at the shipping charges to make sure you're not getting hammered. Once you've considered all this, you can make an informed decision on whether you want to make a bid or not.

Placing your first bid

> *This is where the fun begins*

Nikon D70 Digital SLR Camera Kit		Item number: 3821861456
Includes AF-S DX Zoom-Nikkor 18-70mm Lens		

You are signed in

Add to watch list in My eBay

Current bid: **US $1,126.00**

Place Bid >

Time left: **10 hours 58 mins**
3-day listing
Ends Jun-17-04 15:21:11 PDT
Add to Calendar

↓ Go to larger picture

Start time: Jun-14-04 15:21:11 PDT

History: 43 bids (US $100.00 starting bid)

High bidder: watt_v2001 (0) 8

Item location: West Vancouver
Canada

Ships to: Worldwide

↓ Shipping and payment details

Seller information

marshallalicia3 (0) 8
Feedback Score: 0 feedback reviews
Member since Jun-09-04 in Canada

Read feedback comments

Ask seller a question

View seller's other items

Safe Buying Tips

Description

Item Specifics - Digital Cameras

Digital Camera Type:	SLR, Professional	Optical Zoom:	--
Digital Camera Brand:	Nikon	Manufacturer Warranty:	Yes
Resolution (Megapixels):	6.1 megapixels	Condition:	New, Never Opened

If the picture looks good and you didn't see any details that discouraged you from bidding (like an outrageous shipping price or a picture of a banged-up item), all you have to do is click the Place Bid button (circled in red above) to get into the auction. Well, it's not all you have to do, but it's certainly the first thing you do.

Setting how much you're willing to pay

> *It's time to decide how much this item's really worth to you*

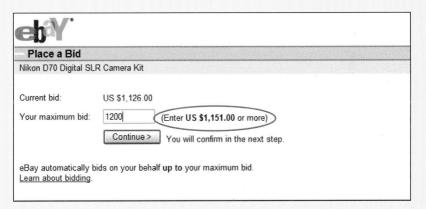

The Place a Bid page is where you decide how much you're willing to bid. The current bid is shown at the top of the page, and obviously you'll need to enter a bid higher than the current bid if you want a chance of winning the auction. eBay has made it so you can't just bid one penny higher than the current bid (in other words, if the current bid is $1,125.00, a bid of $1,125.01 will be automatically rejected). Instead they use bidding increments, and the higher the cost of the item you're bidding on, the larger the increment you have to use. By the way, for the auction shown above, because the current bid is $1,125.00, your minimum bid increment would be $26—eBay automatically calculates that and shows you your minimum bid to the right of the bid field (it appears in parentheses, and is circled above).

> *When it comes to how much you're really willing to pay, eBay can keep a secret*

ebaY®

Place a Bid

Nikon Coolpix 995 3.2 Megapixel

Current bid: US $158.05

Your maximum bid: [   ] (Enter US $160.55 or more)

[Continue >]   You will confirm in the next step.

eBay automatically bids on your behalf **up to** your maximum bid.
Learn about bidding.

If the current bid on that iPod you want is $7, but you'd actually be willing to pay up to $229 for it, then enter $229 as your bid. Although you just told eBay the maximum amount you'd pay, it won't share that information with sellers. Instead, what it does is look at the current bid, and then automatically enters a bid for you that is the current high bid plus the minimum increment. If no one else bids on the item—that's your price (not the $229, so it's yours for a steal). If someone comes in and outbids you, eBay will automatically put in a new bid for you that's one minimum increment higher. It will do this as many times as necessary until the bidding reaches your maximum bid. At that point, if you want to stay in the hunt, you have to increase your maximum bid.

> *eBay keeps you posted on the auction status via email*

You Are the Current High Bidder   eb Y

Dear Stephen,
You are currently the high bidder for the following eBay item from elialbek.

Bid details
Item name:	"NEW" IKEA TABLE LAMP
Item number:	5102526787
Seller:	elialbek
Quantity:	1
Your current bid:	US $15.50
Your maximum bid:	US $16.00
Current price:	US $15.50
End Date:	Jun-18-04 11:00:14 PDT

View the item you're bidding on:
http://cgi.ebay.com/ws/eBayISAPI.dll?ViewItem&item=5102526787&ssPageName=ADME:B:BN:US:1

O nce you've made your bid, you're currently the high bidder. eBay sends you an email with the auction, item number, price, and other information for your records. eBay will also email you if you are outbid by another member, which keeps you from being outbid without knowing about it.

> If you win, eBay will drop you an email to let you know

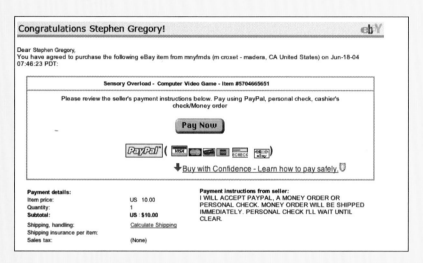

I f it turns out that you've won your eBay auction (the auction time ran out and you had the highest bid), eBay will send you an email telling you you've won. The email will include the price the item went for and the seller's contact information (which is very important). However, winning isn't everything, because now you have to actually contact the seller and arrangement payment and delivery—we'll cover those next.

Hi Frank:
I just won the auction for your 2004 Jaguar XJ-8 and wanted to introduce myself.

I'll be paying by PayPal, and I'd love to have the Jag delivered to my home. Here's my address:

Stephen Gregory
Waldorf Astoria Hotel
Penthouse
301 Park Ave.
New York, NY 10022

You can contact me by phone, by calling 1-800-NICE-TRY

Thanks again, and keep an eye out for that PayPal payment.

Many thanks,

Stephen

After receiving the email about your auction victory, you still have a few tasks left to complete. First you must email the seller (as I mentioned, their contact info is in the email eBay sent to you telling you you've won). Auction etiquette dictates that you, the buyer, must initiate the contact with the seller (by the way, eBay does not do this for you—it sends you the results of the auction then steps aside).

PayPal—the currency of eBay

> *One of the most popular ways to pay on eBay*

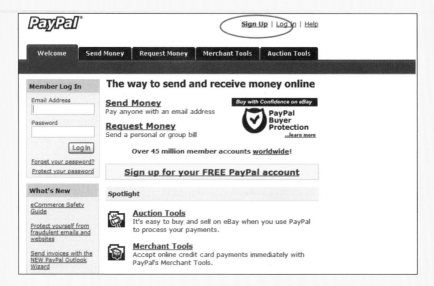

The PayPal service (which is owned by eBay itself) has exploded in popularity recently because it's an easy, secure way to pay for items electronically (they don't share your credit card info with anyone), and it comes with a Buyer Protection plan. To set up a PayPal account, click on the PayPal link at the bottom of eBay's Home page. To set up your account, click the Sign Up link on the top of PayPal's Home page (it's circled in red above) to start the registration process (they're going to ask you the standard stuff—name, address, phone, etc.). Once you get through all that, it will send an email to your email account (for security purposes) and you'll have to click the link in the email to activate your account.

Setting up PayPal for payment

>Once your account is set-up, you have to link it to a credit card or bank

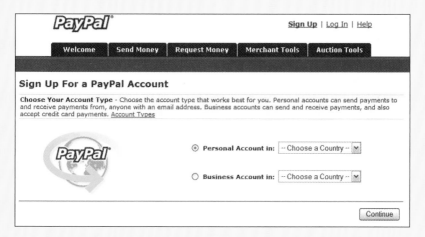

Once your account is active, you'll need to provide PayPal with either a credit card number or bank account number that your PayPal account will be linked to. At this point, you're not spending any money—this is still part of the set-up process. One advantage of using PayPal is that you'll be able to bid on more auctions because although most individual sellers can't accept VISA, Mastercard, or American Express (those are usually accepted only by companies selling on eBay), individuals can set themselves up to accept PayPal fairly easily (in fact, even if they have nothing more than an email account, they can get paid via PayPal).

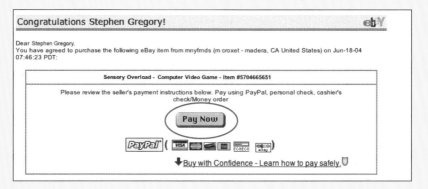

Let's say you've won an auction. When you get the confirmation email, in most cases there will be a "Pay Now" button you can click right within the email confirmation itself (shown circled in red above) that will let you use your PayPal account to pay the seller right on the spot. Just click the button and you'll be directed to a page where you can review your purchase, confirm your shipping address, etc. There's even a Message to Seller field so you can also include a note (perhaps something like "Here's your stinkin' money."). Finally, after confirming all your info, you'll see a "Pay" button. Click that and the seller is paid and informed of all your contact and shipping info, so they can process the transaction and get your goods on the way to you.

> *After you've paid, drop them an email*

Hi Frank:

It's me again. I just made the payment for the Jag via PayPal and you should be seeing a confirmation real soon.

Thanks again and I look forward to seeing those "bling-bling" wheels! :)

Take care,

Stephen Gregory

This is another one of those eBay etiquette things that brings both good karma and positive feedback about you, as a buyer. Even though the seller will get an automated notice once you've paid for the item with PayPal, it's nice just to send a quick email to let them know you've paid via PayPal, and that they should be seeing a transaction soon. Again, just an etiquette thing, but having a good rep on eBay can mean a lot.

> *You start by setting up a Seller's account*

To begin setting up your own auctions and selling your own items on eBay, first you have to register as a seller, so click on the Sell link at the top of eBay's Home page. eBay first asks you to confirm your existing information, then it's going to ask you for your credit card information (you have to provide this before you can sell on eBay). After you provide this, you'll be asked for your checking account info (strictly for security purposes—to keep the riffraff out—they won't deduct money from your checking unless you authorize it first). Once you provide both of those pieces of info, you're ready to start building your own auctions.

> *Before you go much further, make sure you've got some decent photos*

To give your item the best chance of selling, you've got to include a photo—you get to display one photo for free. If you've got a digital camera (or know someone who does), snap a quick photo of your item, save it in JPEG format (most digital cameras create their images as JPEGs), and then upload that photo to your auction page using eBay Picture Services. When you're completing the Sell my item form, you'll see a link for "eBay Picture Services." Adding a photo is critical to the success of your auction, so don't overlook it—it's that important.

A bit about eBay's fees

> *You knew this was too good to be free, right?*

Insertion Fees for Regular, Reserve Price Online Auction, and Multiple Item Listings

U.S.		U.K.	
Starting Price, Opening Value or Reserve Price	Insertion Fee	Opening Value or Reserve Price	Listing Fee
$0.01 - $0.99	$0.30	£0.01 - £0.99	£0.15
$1.00 - $9.99	$0.35	£1.00 - £4.99	£0.20
$10.00 - $24.99	$0.60	£5.00 - £14.99	£0.35
$25.00 - $49.99	$1.20	£15.00 - £29.99	£0.75
$50.00 - $199.99	$2.40	£30.00 - £99.99	£1.50
$200.00 - $499.99	$3.60	£100.00 and up	£2.00
$500.00 and up	$4.80		

Ebay makes its money by charging two small fees: One is for listing your item for sale, and the other is actually a small portion of the final amount of all winning bids. Part of the success of eBay has been that these fees are very small, ranging from about 30¢ on up to $4.80* for expensive items (see the table above). This is pretty much a bargain for sellers, but since eBay collects these fees from millions of transactions, they still make out all right. Once you create an auction and post your item for sale, your confirmation page will summarize the fees charged.

*U.K. residents: eBay.co.uk fees range from 15p up to £2.00.

> *There are four main types of auctions on eBay*

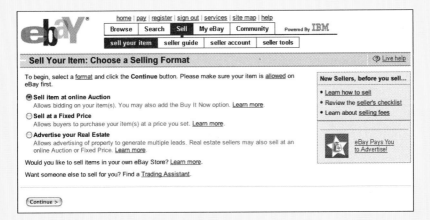

Once you're approved and you start to set up your first auctions, one of the first things that eBay will want to know is which type of auction you will be conducting. There are actually four different auction types. Normal (the one you already know and love), Reserve auctions, Dutch auctions, and Private auctions. In the next few pages, we'll look at each to help you decide which one is right for you.

◉ **Sell item at online Auction**
Allows bidding on your item(s). You may also add the Buy It Now option. <u>Learn more</u>.

○ **Sell at a Fixed Price**
Allows buyers to purchase your item(s) at a price you set. <u>Learn more</u>.

○ **Advertise your Real Estate**
Allows advertising of property to generate multiple leads. Real estate sellers may also sell at an online Auction or Fixed Price. <u>Learn more</u>.

Would you like to sell items in your own eBay Store? <u>Learn more</u>.

Want someone else to sell for you? Find a <u>Trading Assistant</u>.

A normal auction is the most common method used on eBay, or at least it's the one you're probably the most familiar with. A normal auction consists of an opening bid that must be met, a set number of days (on eBay auctions go for 3, 5, 7, or 10 days), and a general progression. People bid, people outbid each other, no funny stuff, no hidden tricks, just the good old-fashioned "I'll pay two dollars more for that rabbit cage than you will" type of auction.

> *If you need to get a certain price, here's how to protect yourself*

Pricing and duration

Starting price ★ Required
$ 99.00
Bidding will begin at your **starting price**.

Reserve price (**fee varies**)
$ 279.00
The lowest price at which you're willing to sell your item is the **reserve price**

Buy It Now price ($0.05)
$
Sell to the first buyer who meets your **Buy It Now price**.

In a Reserve auction the seller has set an amount of money that the bids must meet or exceed for the item to be sold. This reserve is not shown and is kept secret. On the screen you will see next to the current bid the phrase "Reserve Not Met," meaning that the current bid is not sufficient to meet the minimum amount of money the seller has indicated he/she wants. If the reserve is met (or exceeded) the item sells to the highest bidder. When a reserve isn't met, the seller keeps the item. You enter your Reserve price in the Pricing and Duration section of your Sellers form (the form you fill out when you're going to sell something on eBay).

Auction types explained—Dutch (multiple item auctions)

> *Ideal when you've got a bunch of identical items to sell*

Quantity *

Individual Items | NEW! Lots

Number of items *

7

Learn more about **multiple item** listings.

A Dutch auction (technically called a "multiple item auction") is where the seller (you) has more than one of the item you're offering to sell at auction. Let's say for example you have seven identical fish tanks you want to sell. The highest bidder/winner chooses how many fish tanks they want, and they have the choice of taking all seven, or just a few.

> *Use this when you want to hide the identities of your bidders (and the winner)*

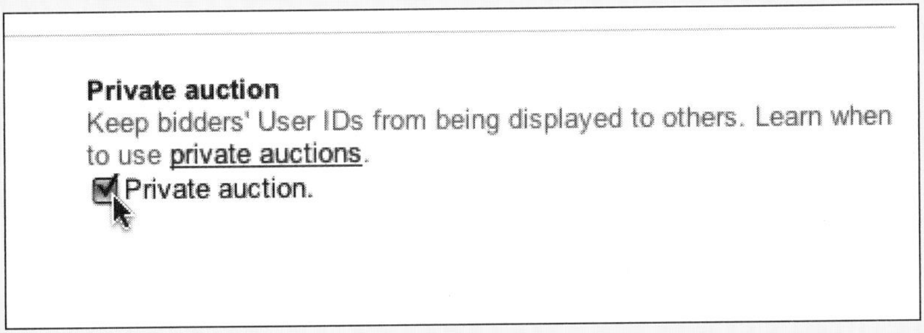

Private auction

Keep bidders' User IDs from being displayed to others. Learn when to use **private auctions**.

☑ Private auction.

This auction progresses as the normal one does, the only difference being that the bidder's identity, and even the auction's winner, is kept secret. Meaning you'll see the current highest bid, but you won't be able to see who it is. This is a smart choice when you feel the people bidding on your particular item may be very seasoned eBay pros—by keeping their identifies secret it may make what could be a nasty bidding war much more friendly (since bidders aren't sure if the person they're bidding against is their "eBay nemesis," or just another nice buyer). You choose the Private auction by clicking the checkbox shown above in the Pricing and Duration section when you're completing your Sellers form.

> *eBay advertising takes many forms*

Increase your item's visibility

☐ Remember my selections in the section below.
Selections will be saved for the next time I list.

Gallery options
This will be displayed as your first picture
⦿ No Gallery picture

○ Gallery ($0.25)
Add a small version of your first pictures to search and listings. See example

○ Gallery Featured ($19.95)
Add a small version of your first pictures to search and listings and showcase your picture in the Featured area of the Gallery View. See

Make your listing stand out
☐ Bold ($1.00)
Attract buyers' attention and set your listing apart in search results - use **bold**. See example

☐ Highlight ($5.00)
Make your listing stand out with a colored band in search results. See example

Promote your listing on eBay
☐ Featured Plus! ($19.95)
Showcase your listing in the Featured area of search and listings. See example

☐ Home Page Featured ($39.95 for 1 item, $79.95 for 2 or more items)
Get maximum exposure! Appear in our Featured area and your item is likely to appear on eBay's Home page. See example

Gift Services
Increase exposure for your gift, promote services, and get an icon.
☐ Show as a gift 🎁($0.25)
Provide cost and details in item description for services offered.
    ☐ Gift wrap/gift card   ☐ Express shipping   ☐ Ship to gift recipient

---

After you've determined the type of auction you want, you'll get an opportunity to stand out a bit from the crowd via Listing Upgrades (little extras you can add to catch a potential buyer's eye). eBay charges extra fees for these Listing Upgrades. In this brief section I'll go over a few of the options to give you a better idea of what you have at your disposal and of some of the benefits of advertising in this fashion.

Go bold for a buck, or try highlighting

> *Standing out can cost just a little more*

Make your listing stand out

☑ Bold ($1.00)

Attract buyers' attention and set your listing apart in search results - use **bold**.

☐ Highlight ($5.00)

Make your listing stand out with a colored band in search results. <u>See example</u>.

When you call up a search you might notice that your eye is instantly drawn to some ads, while others sort of blend into the background. Why is that? If you look again you'll see that some of the titles and ads are set in bold text. eBay charges one dollar for every word you put in bold (so if you're selling an Apple iPod mini, and you want that in bold, it'll cost ya three bucks extra). Not a bad investment considering what a visual difference these bold words make. For five dollars eBay will highlight your entire ad in color to help it catch a potential buyer's eye. This is one of the more expensive Listing Upgrades, so you'll have to decide if this option makes sense for your item.

Having a photo appear with your listing

> *It's the best thing you can do with your spare change*

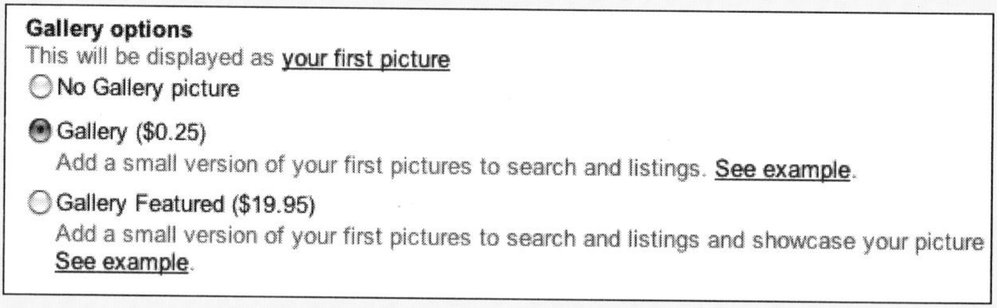

Gallery options
This will be displayed as your first picture
No Gallery picture
Gallery ($0.25)
Add a small version of your first pictures to search and listings. See example.
Gallery Featured ($19.95)
Add a small version of your first pictures to search and listings and showcase your picture
See example.

For a measly 25 cents* you can have a photo of your product appear with your listing. Since a picture tells a thousand words (and people feel so much more comfortable buying something they can see), this is money (OK, spare change) very well spent. To add this, just choose the Listing Upgrade called Gallery (as shown above).

*U.K. residents: 12p

Promote your listing on eBay
Featured Plus! ($19.95)
Requires a feedback rating of 10+. Learn more.

Home Page Featured ($39.95 for 1 item, $79.95 for 2 or more items)
Requires a feedback rating of 10+. Learn more.

For $39.95* eBay will put a rotating link to your auction on the Featured Items section of their Home page (www.eBay.com*). By rotating, I mean that it won't be there all the time—it will appear periodically like a rotating billboard, but it's just a link. Now, I say "just a link" but it's just a link that appears on the Home page of one of the most popular sites on the entire Web, so that's saying something. To choose this Listing Upgrade choose Home Page Featured.

*U.K. residents: £49.95. See www.eBay.co.uk

Putting your auction in the right category

> *Here's how to make it easy to find your auction*

Main category

○ Antiques	Antique silver, furniture, ceramics, textiles & other décor
○ Art	Paintings, prints, photos, posters, folk art & sculpture
○ eBay Motors	Cars, boats, aircraft, motorcycles, parts & accessories
○ Books	Books, textbooks, collectible books, children's books, magazines & more
○ Business & Industrial	Equipment & supplies for Construction, Farm, Restaurant, Retail, Healthcare, Manufacturing, Office and much more
⦿ Cameras & Photo	Cameras, camcorders, lenses, memory, accessories & more
○ Clothing, Shoes & Accessories	Apparel, footwear & accessories
○ Coins	Coins, paper money & numismatic supplies
○ Collectibles	Decorative Collectibles, Coin-Op & Casino, Comics, Militaria, Advertising and more
○ Computers & Networking	Laptops, Desktop PCs, Apple/Macintosh, Printers, Monitors, Software, Wireless & Home Networking, Servers, Routers, Switches, Telephone Systems, Components
○ Consumer Electronics	Cell Phones, Home Theater, MP3 Players, TVs
○ Crafts	Craft supplies of all kinds: Needlearts, Scrapbooking, Painting, Ceramics, Woodworking and more!

Once you've chosen your Listing Upgrades (if any), next click on the Sell tab at the top of the page. This is where you'll choose which category your item should appear within. eBay will walk you through the sub-categories and drop down menus to help you get to just the right category, and this little bit of extra effort on your part can really help drive potential buyers your way. Besides a main category, you might also want to choose one sub-category while you're there (so for example, if you're selling a Nikon D70 digital camera, you'll want to be under Cameras and Photography as your main category, but also in Digital Cameras as a sub-category.

Writing your item's description

> Be honest and thorough and you'll get more interest

Item description *

Be sure to include in your description: Condition (new, used, etc.), original price, and dimensions or size. notable markings or signatures, or its background history. See more tips for <u>Training Equipment</u>.

> The focus pads are in new condition, but the training unit itself has a couple of minor scratches on the left side. There is also one bolt missing on the left side, but it's a standard size and you can find a replacement at Home Depot. Overall, it looks like new, with the exception of those tiny scratches.

Enter <p> to start a new paragraph. Get more <u>HTML tips</u>.

While you're creating your item's description, eBay will give you the opportunity to rate it. Be careful about over-hyping your items, or you can expect a barrage of angry emails from customers that are seriously disappointed. Don't say the item is in Mint Condition if it isn't perfect. Hiding an item's defects or flaws can be the quickest way to get yourself a page full of negative feedback, which will impact your ability to attract buyers in the future.

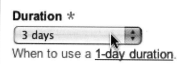

Duration ✳

    3 days   ⬍

When to use a **1-day duration**.

Start time

Listing scheduling requires a **credit card on file**.

Another decision you'll have to make is how long you want your auction to run (your choices are 3, 5, 7, or 10 days), and at what time your auction will end. This is pretty much up to you, and you make your duration decision in the "Sell your Item" form (found in the section for Enter Pictures and Item Details). You choose your duration from the pop-up menu (as shown above).

Setting your shipping policies

> *You'll need to decide who pays the shipping*

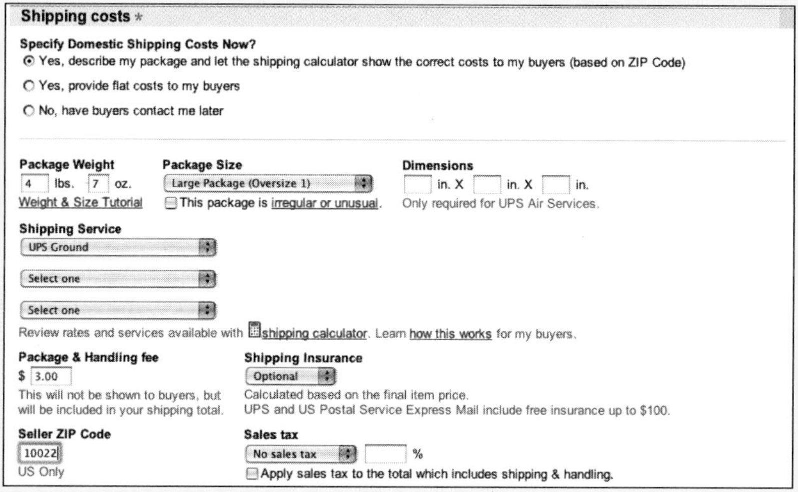

Shipping costs *
Specify Domestic Shipping Costs Now?
Yes, describe my package and let the shipping calculator show the correct costs to my buyers (based on ZIP Code)
Yes, provide flat costs to my buyers
No, have buyers contact me later
Package Weight
4 lbs. 7 oz.
Weight & Size Tutorial
Package Size
Large Package (Oversize 1)
This package is irregular or unusual.
Dimensions
in. X in. X in.
Only required for UPS Air Services.
Shipping Service
UPS Ground
Select one
Select one
Review rates and services available with shipping calculator. Learn how this works for my buyers.
Package & Handling fee
$ 3.00
This will not be shown to buyers, but will be included in your shipping total.
Shipping Insurance
Optional
Calculated based on the final item price.
UPS and US Postal Service Express Mail include free insurance up to $100.
Seller ZIP Code
10022
US Only
Sales tax
No sales tax
%
Apply sales tax to the total which includes shipping & handling.

Another decision you'll need to make during this set-up phase is how to handle shipping (that's right, you'll be shipping the product to your buyer), and because shipping can add considerable cost to the each item, you'll have to decide who pays the shipping costs—you (the seller) or the buyer? If they're paying, are you charging a flat fee, or should they use eBay's shipping cost calculator (based on their ZIP code or Post Code). You'll also have to determine whether you're just shipping domestically, or if you will need to ship internationally. There are checkboxes that will prompt you to make these decisions.

> *Do you have a merchant account or is PayPal better for you?*

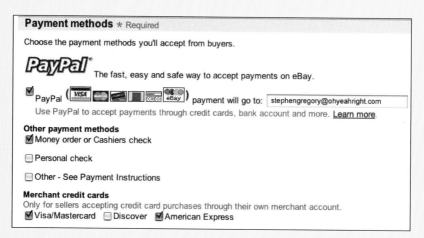

Payment methods * Required

Choose the payment methods you'll accept from buyers.

The fast, easy and safe way to accept payments on eBay.

☑ PayPal (VISA) payment will go to: stephengregory@ohyeahright.com

Use PayPal to accept payments through credit cards, bank account and more. Learn more.

Other payment methods

☑ Money order or Cashiers check

☐ Personal check

☐ Other - See Payment Instructions

Merchant credit cards

Only for sellers accepting credit card purchases through their own merchant account.

☑ Visa/Mastercard ☐ Discover ☑ American Express

Choosing how you'll accept payment has a lot to do with who you are. For example, if you're not a company with a VISA merchant account, you can't accept VISA as a payment option. That's why so many individuals use PayPal, because people can pay you using their credit card, but you get paid directly via PayPal (minus a small processing fee). You can also decide whether you want to accept personal checks, cashiers checks, etc. when setting up your auction. It's pretty much all up to you.

Review your auction before it's posted

> *The last step before your auction goes "live"*

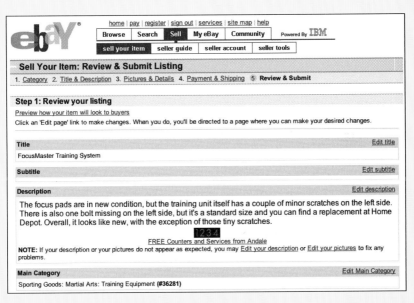

Once you've made all the decisions about your auction and you're ready to "go live" with it, you'll be presented with a Review page displaying a summary of all the information you just entered. Scroll down the page and make sure everything's just the way you want it. When you're sure, click Continue—your auction goes live and you're ready for the bids to come rollin' in. By the way, once you see the auction Review page, eBay will send you an email confirming the auction. eBay loves sending you emails.

Revise Your Item

▶ **Please enter an item number <u>below</u>.**

Revise your listing or add features to attract more buyers
If you want to add more information or features to your listing, just enter your item number and click the Revise Item button below.

If your item has received NO bids or sales and does not end within 12 hours

Revise anything in your listing except the selling format (for example, you can't change your auction item to an eBay Stores item).

If your item has already received a bid/purchase or ends within 12 hours, you can *only*:

- Add to the item description
  (Exception: If your listing already has a bid/purchase AND ends within 12 hours, you **can't** add to your description or add a second category)
- Add optional seller features to increase your item's visibility.

Enter the Item Number: [   ]
(Continue >)

If your auction's underway and you need to make some changes (maybe update the description, hype up the item if you're not getting any bidders, etc.), as long as no one has bid on your item, and it's not less than 12 hours before the end of the auction, eBay will let you change almost anything on your auction page. Here's how: Click on the Sell button on eBay's Home page, then click on the Sell Your Item button. A separate window will open where you'll need to enter your item number, then you'll be able to edit the info. You can also add Listing Upgrades at this time to help you capture some attention.

> *How to keep an eye how things are going*

Change Your Notification Preferences

Notification Methods - Did you know that you can receive instant messages about your eBay activity through party service?

Find out when you've been outbid and when your favorite items appear faster than ever before.

➡ 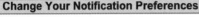Add or change notification services.

(Save Changes)   (Cancel)

Transaction Emails

Note: You cannot opt out of some notifications because they are necessary to provide our services, or a Notification Provider requires you to unsubscribe via their pages(✔).

Status Emails
☑ **Bidding and Selling Daily Status**
    Send me a daily status email of listings on which I am a bidder or seller.

☑ **Item Watch Reminder**
    Send me daily lists of all items in my watch list that will end within 36 hours.

☑ **Bid Notice**
    Notify me when I bid on an item.

☑ **Outbid Notice**
    Notify me when I have been outbid.

If you want to see how things are progressing with your auction, you could just go to that page every day, but there's a more convenient way—have eBay send you a daily status report, which includes how many people have bid and what the current bid is (and when the auction ends). To sign up for this free service, click on the My eBay button at the top of the Home page, then on the left side, under My Account, click on eBay Preferences. Under Notification Preferences, click on View/Change. Next, under Status Emails turn on the checkbox for Bidding and Selling Daily Status (this service is off by default, you have to turn it on). That's it—you'll get an status report emailed to you daily.

> *They don't have your email address, but they can still contact you*

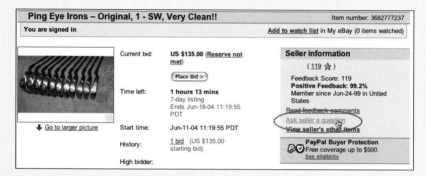

Thankfully, eBay doesn't list your email address on your auction page, but that doesn't mean potential buyers don't have a way to contact you—they just use eBay as the translator. If they want to ask you a question about your item, they can click on the "Ask seller a question" link on the right side of the auction page and they'll be presented with a form where they can ask a question. eBay then forwards that form directly to you. By the way, although bidders can't see your email address, you can see the email address of anyone who bids on your items by clicking on their User ID. Or make their email address visible by turning this feature on in your eBay preferences, under the Modify My Log-In Activities preferences.

> *How to keep from dancing around incessantly*

Please review the seller's payment instructions below. Pay using PayPal, personal check, cashier's check/Money order

Once the auction has ended and you've been informed of the winner's identity, you should drop them a friendly email introducing yourself to help get the ball rolling. (They may send an email to you first, as a matter of etiquette, but it doesn't hurt for you to send one too, even though everybody gets an automated notification from eBay.) In this email, include the amount of their winning bid, how much shipping charges will be, and the total price out the door. You can also remind them of how to make payment (PayPal info, etc.) and ask them to confirm how they're paying and where they'd like the item shipped. If you're uncomfortable with all this, you might enjoy eBay's own free automated invoicing service called Checkout. This feature sends the winner an email with the total and your PayPal payment info, and a link to Checkout so they can pay right there and then. Then, when they pay, it sends you an email with their payment info and shipping address.

Index